A Wonderful Bigness

For Annabelle and Benjamin, you come from great people. Love, Auntie Di

And for my mother, Kay, who shares her wonderful bigness with everyone. I love you.

~DD

To my parents, Gwen and David, who have always encouraged me to draw in the margins, and to my wife Tina, who knows all about big families and big hearts.

~BA

Based on the stage show "If a Place Could Be Made" by Diana Daly, Louise Moyes, and Anne Troake

This is a love story.

It's a large tale, and a true tale—about loving your family, loving your friends, and loving yourself.

It starts, for our purposes anyhow, in a beautiful part of the island of Newfoundland: St. Mary's, St. Mary's Bay. Most settlers in the bay were of Irish descent; they kept their heritage intact by telling stories, singing songs, and using the skills and knowledge that had been passed down to them. This is where my family, the Dalys, are from. I'd like to introduce them to you.

So, here we go, up the Salmonier Line, out the Irish Loop, to the gently rolling hills and waters of St. Mary's Bay. Make sure to put some bread in your pockets to ward off the faeries! It was not so very long ago, but long enough for the world to be very different than it is today: there was no internet, there were no televisions or telephones, no grocery stores or malls, but there was a strapping young man from Riverhead named Daniel Daly.

Daniel was a policeman, big and strong; he was the only policeman for the entire shore. He fell in love with a young woman named Kitty Ryan, who was also from Riverhead. She had a way about her, Kitty did, a wonderful bigness Daniel used to say. "There's a wonderful bigness about you, Kitty," he'd say. And, sure, she fell in love with him too.

I always imagine Daniel courting Kitty with a song. Let's listen in on a song he might have written for her:

Kitty Darlin'

There's a wonderful bigness to you, maid,
Kitty darlin, Kitty dear.
Let's fill our house with children
And always keep them near.

There's a wonderful lightness to you, dear,
Kitty darlin, Kitty dove.
What an honour to call you Mo'Cuishle,
For my heart pulses with your love.

Will ye fast yer hand to mine, girl?
Kitty darlin, Kitty sweet?
I'll protect you for life, if you'll be my wife,
And the circle we'll complete.

I'll give you a garden, I'll build you a house,
Kitty darlin, Kitty dear.
And we'll practice our faith
With a family so great,
And we'll always keep them near.

special dispensation
Kitty & Daniel

Kitty and Daniel—these were my great grandparents.

They welcomed life with open arms, and life gave them a lot to welcome. They married, moved down the road to St. Mary's proper, and had twelve children.

The first of those children was born in 1914 and he was my grandfather, William Joseph Daly, who grew up to be Constable Bill Daly of the Royal Newfoundland Constabulary and the best poppy anyone could have ever asked for. I loved him so much. He was my mom's father, and he was a great big man, over six feet tall with hands so big people called them "hams." His hands were as big as hams! Not really, but pretty close. Those hands built boats, fences, houses, highways, and roofs; they planted gardens, installed plumbing, arrested men, broke bones, made furniture, dried tears, and slammed cards onto the table so hard all four legs jumped off the floor. He was an everyman, a policeman, a Catholic man, a provider, a brother, a father, a husband, a dancer, a storyteller, a philosopher, a poet, and a listener; generous with his time, his strength, and his talents. He could grow anything in his garden—he had a green thumb. A large green thumb! He told great stories, and he always took care of those he loved. But my great big poppy was a little baby once, and he was Kitty and Daniel's pride and joy.

Soon another baby was on the way. Now, during this pregnancy, Kitty said she felt no different than with her first, but this baby, my great-uncle Mike, was born small. The next child, my great-aunt Ann, was born small too, with legs it's hard to describe, except to say that she hardly had any at all. Then there was a third small baby, my great-aunt Rose. And while they were delighted by all their children, and loved them dearly, Kitty and Daniel started to wonder if they had done something wrong to cause these babies to be born so small.

And so Kitty travelled to St. John's, the capital city, to see the archbishop, the holiest man she knew of, besides the pope, to ask his advice. As Catholics, it was their duty to have lots of children, but why was God sending them these small babies?

"Holy Father," she asked, "why do you think I am having these small, small children? Have we done something wrong? What should I do?"

And, as men like that often do, the holy man answered with a question: "What do you think GOD would want you to do????"

She thought about it, and thought about it, and then, "Have children," she said.

The archbishop offered Kitty special dispensation not to have any more babies—which was a very big deal back then—but she declined.

"I think God wants me to have a big family," she said. "We will take care of every child that He gives us. If a place can be made for them, it will be."

All told, Kitty and Daniel had Bill, Mike, Ann, Rose, Theresa, Gordon, Mary, Tom, Cack, Joe, and Daniel. There was little Peter too; he died of scarlet fever, as was so common in those days. But this is not Peter's story—some stories are too sad to tell.

Of Kitty and Daniel's children, six were tall, and six were small. My great-aunties and great-uncles Mike, Ann, Rose, Joe, Mary, and Cack each had skeletal dysplasia, in one form or another. Ann and Rose quite likely also had osteogenesis imperfecta, or brittle bone syndrome, and that is why they were so much smaller even than their small siblings. At that time, they would have been called "dwarves," but nowadays, respectfully, we say "little people" or "persons of short stature." It is best to ask the person which term they prefer.

How could a family bear the challenges—one child who died, six children who had health issues and whom others would call "freaks," neighbours gossiping about how they must be hexed? And yet they were still so full of love, of that wonderful bigness Daniel first saw in Kitty. Sounds like a fairy tale, doesn't it? It wasn't, not really. But in a way, as you'll see, there is happy ending.

Big or small, every one of Kitty and Daniel's children was treated equally. They were never coddled; all of the children were given chores to do to the best of their abilities. While my grandfather Bill would work in the garden, build fences, and help with the livestock, Mike and Joe would make furniture or fish—they were great boatsmen; Mary, Cack, and Ann would help with the cooking and cleaning, sew clothes for themselves, and make dolls out of their mother's discarded gloves and scraps of material; Rose would make beautiful greeting cards.

And as they grew older, each continued to contribute to the health and happiness of the household. For example, my pop, being the oldest and very big and strong, worked to bring home money for the family. This was the Great Depression, and times were hard for most everyone. When he was just eighteen he travelled to Corner Brook, on the other side of the island, to join a work crew and build the highway. He sent every one of his cheques home so that the family could buy a horse. He became a member of the Royal Newfoundland Constabulary, just like his father, when he turned twenty-five. They were all so proud!

Aside from his profession, Pop was always working in the garden, planting onions, cabbage, potatoes, peas, carrots, strawberries; you name it, he could grow it. Rows upon rows of food. And flowers. Oh, the flowers! Gladioli, roses, peonies, marigolds… And he was a dab hand at building and fixing things around the house, like keeping the fences painted a crisp white, making sure the steps were sturdy and the railings strong. One stormy spring night he had to go out to the barn to help their sheep birthing lambs. It was one of those nasty Sheila's Brush storms with snow whipping around in all directions. He tucked his head down and made it from the house to the barn, and sensed right away something was wrong. One little newborn was doing poorly. It wasn't eating; in fact, it was limp and near lifeless. Pop tucked the creature into his coat and found his way back to the house to give it to his mother to see if she could help. In the kitchen she set the little lamb in a box and put it under their Waterloo Stove where it was sure to be warm. The little animal held on through the night and was soon strong enough to go back out to its mother.

People had different knowledge back then. For example, when my pop accidentally cut his thumb straight down the middle of the nail with his axe, his mother knew just what to do. She sewed it together with a strand of her hair and applied some cobwebs that had collected in the corner to help heal the wound. She understood the healing properties of penicillin before knowing that it was a medical breakthrough! And Pop always remembered too; he had a big scar line down his thumb to remind him.

My great-aunt Theresa was the only daughter who was not small. In those days, women's work in a household never seemed to end. While Mary, Cack, Ann, and Rose all worked in the garden and the kitchen, and tended to each other's bathing and grooming as best they could, Theresa had a considerable amount of work to do to help her mother, especially with cleaning, mending, sewing, gardening, attending at births, making meals, and preserving food for such a large family.

The family devised ways to work with my great-aunties' and -uncles' physical challenges. Mike and Joe built furniture that was just the right size for the smaller Dalys. As his brothers and sisters aged, and needed wheelchairs instead of crutches, my pop became an expert ramp builder.

There is a part of the health and happiness of a home that can't be built with physical things: humour, poetry, community, laughter, art, music, dancing—all helped ease the hardship and boredom of long cold winters, too little food, and too much illness. Everyone contributed wit and spirits, so the mood at home was always lively.

Kitty and Daniel Daly had great courage, great faith, and great good humour. They loved all their children dearly. Some of their children stayed with them their entire life. It was a blessing to have them under the same roof. Some of their children moved away. And some of their children had their own children, and sure, those grandchildren, like my mom and her sister, would go and live with them, too, sometimes!

A house full of Love

When they were courting, Daniel promised Kitty a house full of love, and that's what he gave her. If we were to peek in the window of their big house in St. Mary's, through the lacy curtain, past the African violets on the windowsill, we would see the Dalys' home full of fun and intellect, of poetry and culture, of hard workers and clever minds, of music and craft, of respect and support. Let's imagine that we are going up the steps to go in and say hello. Always and ever, there'd be a warm welcome for any friend or visitor: a loud chorus of "HOW ARE YE?" and huge smiles all around. Someone would, for sure, make tea. Kitty would ask how your family was, Mary and Cack would want to know all the gossip, Joe would probably have a joke for you… Everyone would be included.

The Dalys were Irish Catholics, and religion was central in their lives. Their faith helped them face life's trials, and treasure all the good that accompanied the bad. In those days, and in that place, a policeman sometimes had a few jail cells at his house in case he needed to bring any criminals into court. They would spend the night in the cells and carry on to St. John's in the morning. Daniel was the policeman for the whole shore, and he and Kitty had two jail cells on the back of their house.

Kitty would feed the inmates, Mary and Cack would read any letters they had for them, and every evening, when the family said the rosary, whoever was in those cells would be brought into the house to pray. No matter what their morals or beliefs, they were told firmly to "come in, and get down on yer benders." No arguments allowed.

Let's sit in with them while they pray. Everyone is very focused. There is no joking now, no fooling around. Pop's voice booms out the beginning of the Hail Mary and all the others join the second part. "Holy Mary, mother of God…" ten times. Settle into a rhythm. Over and over again. "The fifth Glorious Mystery…" The rosary beads click and rub in fingers, absorbing the intention behind the prayers. Pomegranate red, sky blue, clear crystal, Connemara Marble. Each set is special to its owner. Everyone's voice is important and everyone's voice is equal, because every one of us is capable of redemption. Even those "official" guests.

Joe
HOHNER

Idle Idle Idle: Meet my great-uncle Joe

So, here we are in St. Mary's: it is summertime—fresh air, open fields, the sun shining! FREEDOM! Let's get to know Joe a little bit. My great-aunties and great-uncles were very clever, especially Joe. He was an "ideas" guy. In St. Mary's, everyone described him as "idle." That meant, if he wasn't occupied, he was busy looking for trouble.

Joe was strong and athletic, but he was born with his feet facing each other; so he had to get around on crutches. And could he go on them! In the summertime, kids would run and play all over the hills, meadows, and beaches of St. Mary's. But even with his crutches, Joe couldn't go as fast as the boys with legs that didn't face in. So he set to work and built himself a go-kart for getting around; he called it a "trolley." He and the boys would go tearing about. They could get up to great speeds. Sometimes Joe would steer straight for the cow patties so that whoever was pushing the go-kart from behind (usually Alistair Ryan) would step right in the poop! (hahahahah!)

When she was only a very little girl, my mom would be sent down to the wharf by Joe with a little bucket to collect "fish blubber," fish oil he used to grease the go-kart's axle. That was a long time ago, but she still remembers—it stank! (Pahyouhay!!)

Now, Mary and Cack, Joe's sisters, were very into fashion; they made their own clothes and they loved to get dressed up. They would have fancy picnics on the beach. One day, they had worked extra hard to prepare for one of their picnics. They made new dresses with perfect ruffles; they donned perfect hats and gloves. They cut sandwiches into perfect triangles; they spread a beautiful tablecloth, and laid out fresh hankies. Everything was just so. Bliss.

That's when Joe and the boys spied them from up on the hill, and started bawling out, "Give us a samwich!!!"

Annoyed, yet dignified, the girls bellowed back, "NO!!"

But the boys kept on calling, "CommmmeeeeON, Give us a SAAAAAMMMMM-WWWWIIIICCCCHHH!!!!!"

Mary and Cack sighed, took deep breaths, very calmly settled their tea cups on their saucers, and hollered back, "NO! BUZZ OFF!!!"

And so the boys did buzz off. They buzzed away and found an old tire and some fresh cow dung. Joe and the boys filled that tire with the dung, brought it back to the top of the hill, aimed it at the picnic, and let it fly! And with every bump that tire hit on the way down WET COW POOP sprayed everywhere!!! All over Mary and Cack's new dresses with the perfect ruffles, all over Mary and Cack's perfect hats, all over Mary and Cack's sandwiches cut into perfect triangles.....all over their perfect picnic.

Were Mary and Cack mad?

You bet!
Ever hear the phrase "I'm so mad I could spit!"?
Well, they were that. Hoppin mad, fit to be tied, off their heads, steam coming out of their ears, tears stinging their eyes, seeing red, ROYALLY TICKED!

But it was hard to stay mad at Joe for long, because, oh, he was such a charmer. And handsome? Gorgeous! And a wiz with baseball and hockey statistics—as if he had a photographic memory. He was so much fun! A real divilskin.

He was always coming up with some sort of mischief. Like the time he decided to scare the old fella down the lane. I have no idea what this man did to become the target of Joe's scheme—whatever it was, Joe used all his idle wits to come up with some plan! There were no streetlights back then; out around the bay, nighttime was very dark. And there were always lots of the discarded bits of fish down on the flakes left over from filleting. The boys, being resourceful, decided to improvise with the materials at hand. Joe knew the old fella walked up the lane at a certain time every evening so, with the help of his buddy, he strung a bunch of fish eyes on a line and laid it on the ground across the lane. Fish eyes glow in the dark, you know. Joe and his buddy hid on either side of the lane, waiting for the codger to come. When the old fella got close, they pulled the line taut—ZING!!! All these creepy glowing eyes flashed in front of him and scared the daylights outta him! The boys peeled with laughter, delighted with themselves.

Joe never grew out of that mischievousness either. In the quiet afternoons, Kitty'd be in her chair reading intently, grasping the paper-thin pages of her bible. Tick tock goes the clock. Drip drop goes the faucet. Inhale exhale. Then WHAM! Joe's crutch reaches out and whacks the side of her chair, causing her to startle and rip the page! "Oh Joe, honey! Ye startled me!" Kitty would say. She kept a roll of tape next to her chair for this very purpose. Her bible was full of ripped pages taped together.

Best of all, Joe was musical. He'd practice his accordion for an hour every morning, and the music carried out the window and over the fields. It was a good thing Joe practiced every day, because, in St. Mary's, the Dalys' house was where the parties were held. And the room in the back of the house is where Kitty and Daniel taught them all how to dance. People would come from miles around to laugh, play cards, and dance the Lancers.

Let's go to one of these nights. There's magic in the air! The stars are gorgeous and there is just a breath of breeze. Laughter and music are calling us in the back door. Kitty and Daniel are showing us how it's done. All our friends are piled into the room, and the floor boards are bouncing with all the fine dancing going on. Through the woods! Thread the needle! Ladies step out and crack the whip! Isn't Pop gorgeous when the men step out? They are all so handsome and lively. What wonderful dancers!

Joe is playing jigs and reels, sets and waltzes, tune after tune, late into the night. And they think we don't know, but Rose Marie and little Catherine Ann, who are supposed to be in bed asleep, are spying on the adults. They have their little faces peeking through the hole in the floor that lets the heat up from the downstairs, watching the dancers late into the night.

All of my great aunties and uncles understood that little children would be curious. They were very patient when children wondered about their size, and always had time for questions. When a little girl walked up to my Aunt Ann's wheelchair and asked, "How come you are so small?" instead of getting angry, Aunt Ann replied, "Well, my dear, God took me out of the oven before I was finished baking."

Once, my little brother (who was about four or five at the time) was sitting on the veranda with Uncle Joe and said to him, "Uncle Joe, that must have been some storm!" And Uncle Joe, leaning on his crutches, asked, "Now, what storm was that m'son?" And my brother replied, "Well, the one that blew yer legs that way Uncle Joe!" And Joe didn't miss a beat: "Oh THAT storm!!" he said. "Yes my son, well that storm was SO BIG and SO STRONG,

it blew in through St. Mary's…and blew me legs backwards!"

Come into the Parlour
LONG'S HILL

The family continued to grow and change. By the 1950s some children went off to work, some got married and had children of their own, some stayed and thrived with Kitty and Daniel. And the Dalys did what a lot of Newfoundlanders had to do in those days—they moved to "town"; they left rural Newfoundland in the winter for the big city of St. John's. First they moved to a house on the top of Long's Hill, #77. This house was four storeys high! The bedrooms were on the higher levels and the kitchen down below. But that didn't deter Kitty. The house was still always full of people—family, boarders, and visitors. Ann and Rose had a hard time getting around because of their legs. Ann could scooch down stairs on her bum but she couldn't go back up, and Rose couldn't do either of those things, so Kitty would scoop them up in her arms and carry them. There was a big window at the top of those stairs that looked out over the rooftops of the houses all the way down to the harbour, and windows at the front of the house where you could sit and watch all the activity on the street. The front windows had Kitty's African violets on the sills, and she'd bless them every night with holy water before the house went to sleep. "Good night, God bless ye," sprinkle sprinkle.

Like its name suggests, Long's Hill is suuuuuper long! It used to connect the lower town to the upper town. Everyone had to hoof it up and down Long's Hill to get to where they were going, crutches or not, just like the rest of the neighbourhood. Everyone, that is, except Ann and Rose. They didn't go out very much at all when they lived on Long's Hill. It was just too much of a challenge for them. Some people say that they were "shut in" but I think "housebound" is the more appropriate word. That is another reason why it was so important for everyone to go back to St. Mary's for the summer. Ann and Rose would take the bay taxi with the rest of the family: there they had more options for enjoying the outdoors.

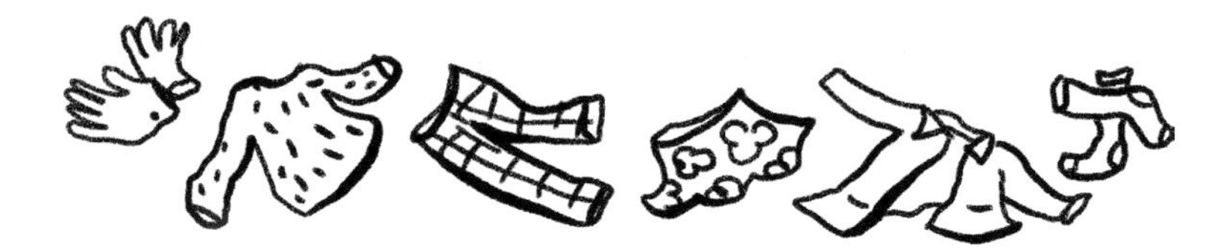

There were no stores where you could go to buy clothes for little people in those days; it was up to the family to make sure everyone was turned out and looking their best. Mary, Ann, and Cack would knit and sew outfits

for each other, and for Rose, Mike, and Joe too. So they were always looking sharp. Mike was an excellent knitter, hair cutter, and tailor. He would tailor all of his own and his brothers' suits, and suits for his nephews and friends too. He had a little shop across from the house on Long's Hill.

Everyone did what they could to contribute to the house and protect the people in it. Grandma Kitty used to take a break in the afternoons and sit on Joe's bed, over which she had hung a picture of the sacred heart of Jesus, to pray. She was praying away one afternoon and happened to look up and notice that Jesus looked different somehow. When she got up close, she saw that Jesus had been replaced by Rocky Marciano, the current world heavy weight boxing champion (and Joe's hero)! She blessed herself and kept on with her prayers. After all, Joe needed 'em.

Eventually, the family moved to a spacious and welcoming farm-style two-storey house on Waterford Bridge Road, across from Bowring Park. It had a large veranda that wrapped around the front…sure, let's pop in for a visit. No one is sitting out on the veranda right now—they must all be inside. Just past the porch full of coats and shoes and crutches and wheelchairs, we go into the huge living room with couches, a television, and the dining table. Those three fancy lady figurines are on the mantle. There's Uncle Joe watching baseball. He's in his wheelchair—it's always parked there next to Ann's chair—and he's leaning on his crutches with a great big toothy grin. He has one of those jelly fruit candies for us. Uncle Mike is watching the game at the table with Father Molloy. Aunt Ann isn't in her usual red sofa chair, so she must be visiting with someone in her room. Out back in the kitchen, Mary and Cack will be playing Crazy Eights with Tony or Dot. Yes, Dot it is. Smells nice in there. A lovely breeze is coming in the back door, the leaves are rich and green on the trees outside, and Irish music is playing on the radio. The old Frigidaire is HUGE and the three little mice magnets are there for you to play with. Everyone is happy to see us. The family's caretaker and dear friend Donna is there, and she gets us a ginger ale.

Ah! Aunt Ann is, indeed, in her room, and we can go in for a visit. Her floor is that sparkly battleship linoleum with blue and gold stars. She has a tiny present for us—a little red kitten pin for your sweater. Mike and Joe's room is further down the hall, past the bathroom. It has wooden paneling on the walls and red plaid bedspreads, and hanging on the wall there is a fabulous picture of a stallion that Uncle Mike drew. There's another picture on the wall that my sister drew for Mike. It is also of a horse, but this one has a cloud with a smiley face and a rainbow coming out of it. Mary and Cack's room is upstairs; now, knowing how glamorous and fun they are, you can imagine what that's like!

Like all of their homes, this new house was always full of love and light and babies and card games and wheelchairs and Purity syrup. Every Christmas Eve, the entire extended family would gather, and a priest would offer Christmas mass in the living room. I'll bring you with me for one of these magical nights. There's the dining table—it's been turned into an altar and the house has become our church. Mary and Cack have ironed and set the holy cloth; the young priest, Robert Ryan, is here, and so is his mother, Roz. The tree is lit, and the fake fire log is plugged in and rolling. We are a little congregation of our own—mothers, fathers, sisters, brothers, aunties, uncles, cousins, grandchildren, grandparents, and friends. Big and small. Everyone is happy to be together and to have such wonderful people in our lives. Beyond the window, it could be blowing a gale outside or snow could be falling, but we are safe and warm. Those were the most special Christmas Eves imaginable.

This house on Waterford Bridge Road was right next to Corpus Christi Church, so why we didn't go there to have Christmas Eve Mass? This was something special that the priests agreed to do with our family. Getting the entire family over to church and back again in winter would have been a large undertaking, and besides, the rest of the parishioners filled those seats in the pews. The priests would come over after giving mass at the church. It was such a gift for us all.

Rose

A Delicate Flower: Meet my great-aunt Rose

Now it's time to meet my great-aunt Rose. Of all of my great-aunties and great-uncles, Rose was the smallest. Everyone who knew her loved her—she was a beautiful, delicate woman with a gorgeous smile. No one knows exactly what her medical condition was, but after she was about seven years old, she could no longer walk. Before that, Aunt Theresa said she was such a swift little kid, there was no catching her! When she was a child, my mother was given the job, whilst visiting, of carrying her aunt Rose from room to room, wherever she wanted to go. This was a very important job for my mom and she made sure to take great care of her auntie. Of course, they would have tons of fun together. They'd go here and there, front room to the back room, out to the veranda, maybe up for a nap on the bed under the open window.

On fine days, Rose liked to sit out on the veranda in a little rocking chair that Mike and Joe had made specially for her, and she would cut out the flowers from greeting cards that people saved for her. Because her hands didn't work so well, Rose used her chin to help guide the scissors. She would cut those flowers out perfectly. Stems, leaves, and all. Then she would glue those delicate paper flowers to old x-ray film and fashion them into flower vases. My family calls them Rose's "Jardineers."

Later in her life, like the Lady of Shalott, Rose saw the world through a mirror. By then, she had such limited mobility that, to be comfortable in her room, she would sit in her chair with her elbow positioned on her bed "just so" for balance. She couldn't turn to see who would come in her room, she couldn't turn to say hello, but she could look into her little jewelry box mirror and see them. And they, in turn, could see her radiant smile and her kind and gentle eyes. That jewelry box mirror was her window on the world. She'd even watch television in the mirror!

A month after Daniel died, Kitty was taken to hospital; she was very ill with the cancer, and in great pain. She couldn't swallow and had to be fed through a tube; she was hooked up to all sorts of devices to give her medicine and monitor her health. Imagine the sadness in the Daly household. They had just lost their father and their mother was dying. Then, Rose took ill as well. She was so ill, in fact, that plans were made to move her out of the house to the hospital. She, who had not been outside their home for years and years, who had to look at the world through a mirror, was leaving.

Mary had been Rose's nurse, like the good sister she was. The night before she was to go to hospital, Mary said to Rose in a half-joking way, "You'll have a big adventure tomorrow, Rose. Those doctors won't believe what's coming!"

Rose, always thinking of others, replied, "Whatever I have to take, I will bear it. I just want God to take some of the pain away from Mom."

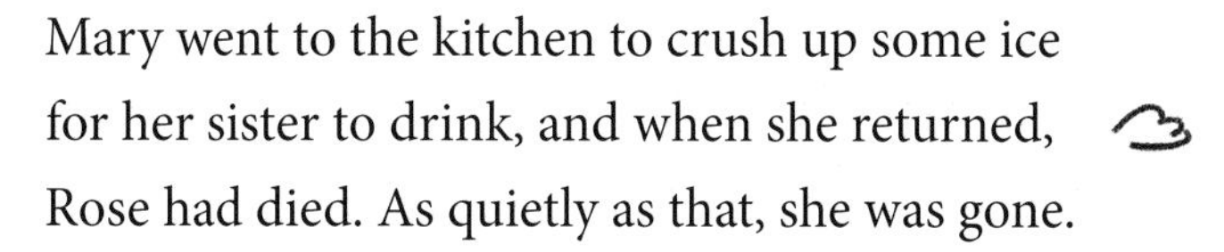

Mary went to the kitchen to crush up some ice for her sister to drink, and when she returned, Rose had died. As quietly as that, she was gone.

My pop, Bill, went into the hospital to give his mother Kitty the news. He was surprised to find that, for the first time in a long time, she seemed in less pain and was able to talk. Before he even had a chance to speak, she said, "Rosie's gone, isn't she?"

"Yes," he replied.

"Well," she said, with a heavy sigh, "I know that Dad is there in Heaven waiting for her with a big smile, but, oh, I would have loved to have held her in my arms one more time."

Then, to Pop's surprise, Kitty asked for a glass of water, and she drank it, no problem. She had a glass of juice, and she drank that, no problem. She had a cup of tea! And then she asked to go to the bathroom. Within a couple of days all of the tubes that had been keeping her alive were taken out.

A week later Kitty was back home, eating her favourite meal of fried fish heads, sitting up at the head of her own table. And she continued to sit there for her meals every day for four more years. It seemed like a miracle, like Rose's last gift of beauty. Rose, who could not go anywhere on her own, somehow seemed to take that last lonely journey in her mother's stead.

Mike

A Brilliant Mind: Meet my great-uncle Mike

After Kitty and Daniel died, Mike became the head of the household. Uncle Mike was warm, and he was handsome. Let's go visit him now. Be prepared—he is going to hug and kiss you so hard, and exclaim, "Yer GORGEOUS!" At least, that's how he always welcomes me, which is kind of embarrassing but also kind of nice. (These days, I do that to my own niece and nephew.) Uncle Mike can spin nickels, and he might take us for a ride to Bowring Park on his motorized wheelchair. I knew him the way a little girl knows a great uncle, but I've come to learn that more than a nickel-spinning, wheelchair-rider—he was a tailor and a shopkeeper. His was the neighbourhood shop on Long's Hill; it sold a few groceries, household items, cigarettes, and candy. (Everybody smoked then; I told you the world was different than it is today!)

He had a brilliant mind—he wrote poetry and was even a member of MENSA. He was what you call "an autodidact," which means he studied and learned on his own, without the help of a teacher. He was great friends with many learned priests. They would sit for hours debating deep existential questions such as: What does God want from us? Is there such a thing as a parallel universe? Is suffering necessary to achieve holiness? Will the Maple Leafs take the Stanley Cup, or the Montreal Canadiens?

The family says he had a love; Mike and his sweetheart, they spent time together and wrote each other long letters. But in those days the stigma of a woman marrying a man with a disability as visible as Mike's was just too great.

Eventually his sweetheart moved away, and Uncle Mike remained what he was: a modern, stylish, cultivated bachelor. And he continued to protect and provide for his brother and sisters, his nieces and nephews, and his treasured friends.

One reason my family doesn't know why they had so many children with skeletal dysplasia—it is incredibly rare to have so many cases in one family—is that Uncle Mike refused to allow anyone to study them. They were not science experiments, he insisted, not oddities to be put on display. Many people with the same conditions in those days did not have such protection, and were subjected to humiliating experiments and studies, as if they were not worthy and equal human beings. That was not happening to his family.

Uncle Mike was a protector and a provider, a philosopher and a poet; I would love to know him now that I am grown. I bet we would have great conversations.

Ann

The Serious Mother: Meet my great-aunt Ann

Aunt Ann was the matriarch of these siblings. The second mother; the serious mother. She was the eldest daughter and had all the responsibilities that any eldest daughter would have. She was pious, and she was in charge. She took a real interest in all her great-nieces and great-nephews. She loved us dearly, and we loved her in return, even if we were a little scared of her sometimes. She loved Gordon Lightfoot's music too. Who doesn't?

Even when she was very young, Ann bossed everyone around, but she hated to be ordered about herself. One day she was sent out to weed the vegetable garden, and she was mad, mad, MAD.

The weeds were so high they towered over her head, but she tore them out of the drills with fervour, gritting her teeth and grumbling, "Who do they think they are?!?" When she had finished the rows, her mother was waiting for her, right proud. "Great job, Ann. Come into the house now. While you were weeding, I got a dress made for you to go to the dance."

Ann used a wicker stroller, a red perambulator with a curved handle, much like a carriage, for transportation. It was a handy thing for getting around, and very useful. She could have her lipstick and smokes tucked in by her feet, best kind, for going to the dances. And just the way she'd tuck those necessaries in by her feet, Ann would tuck away whatever you told her. She was a keeper of secrets. You could tell her anything.

As an adult, Ann made many pilgrimages to Sainte-Anne-de-Beaupré, the church in Québec famous for miracles. My mom accompanied her almost every year.

The altar there is full of crutches and wheelchairs and other tools used to aid people with disabilities; the suggestion being that, after praying at this very special shrine, people would be cured. Who can say? Aunt Ann's legs never grew and she always needed her wheelchair, but she loved going to Sainte-Anne-de-Beaupré and said it was where she felt closest to God.

There she met many people, and her wisdom helped many of them with their problems. People seemed drawn to her for advice and counsel, and she would always comfort and help set them on their path again. One man was so grateful to her for helping him work through his worries that he gifted her a tiny gold medallion with Sainte-Anne-de-Beaupré on it. He had no idea that she had wanted to own it for years, but could never justify the expense of it. She wore that medal for the rest of her life.

One time, before a trip to Sainte-Anne's, she had made herself a new outfit—a beautiful cotton dress, trimmed with lace, long enough for the skirt to drape over the front of her wheelchair—and she came out into the living room to show her brothers and sisters. They all agreed how nice it was. "You look lovely, doesn't she look lovely?" they said. And Joe, the divilskin, added, "Yes. And if you come back from Sainte-Anne's and that skirt's a MINI skirt??? I'M GOIN' WITH YA NEXT YEAR!!!"

Like all the siblings, Ann accepted her condition and made a rich and meaningful life for herself. But once, she did confide to a dear friend, that, as content as she was with her life, there was one thing that she longed for: to know what it felt like—grass beneath her feet and tickling her toes, wind ruffling her hair, sweet smell of wildflowers, warm sun on her upturned face—to run barefoot through a meadow.

Mary & Cack

The Glamour Girls:

My great-aunties and -uncles had many wonderful friends: musicians and thinkers and community workers and teachers. The list is long. Still to this day, if I am somewhere and I mention who my people are, folks remember. They'll say "Oh! I knew them! They always came to the shows!" Or "Those two women went everywhere! They were so stylish!" Or "The Dalys?? I spent many an evening with them. Wonderful people, WONDERFUL people!!"

One of their friends, Ralph O'Brien, sang beautiful Irish ballads; Mary and Cack always had front row seats to his live shows. In fact, they went to ALL the shows during the Irish music revival in the 70s: Tommy Makem, the Clancy Brothers, Gordon Lightfoot, the Sons of Erin, and the Carlton Show Band. They were huge fans and always went backstage to hang out after the shows. We have pictures!

Mary and Cack, in particular, were always together, so if you went in to visit, you visited both of them. And they talked at the same time so you kind of melded the conversation together…it just worked. If we went in to have a visit with them now we'd hear: "There she is! There's our Diana! Oh, and she's brought her friends, come in, come in how are ye?" After grilling all of you on who you are, who raised ye, where your family is from, then we'd probably start talking about all the fun they'd have down at Erin's Pub or the time Mary and Cack were on TV for an Irish special. They went for the music, but, they said, the next thing they knew Ralph put them on the stage and then the cameras started rolling.

They were a riot! My first "rock-star moment" ever was at the Corpus Christi Christmas Pageant. I was five years old and Cabbage Patch Kids were a huge craze. Every kid had one and it was all anyone could talk about. (Mine was named "Hillary Ruby" and she had orange hair.)

Meet my great-aunties Mary and Cack

The lights dimmed, the red curtains opened, and there on the stage was a grown woman playing the part of a little girl. Next to her was a HUGE pile of fresh cabbage leaves. “Wah! Wah! Wah!” she cried, “I wants a Cabbage Patch!” And with that, the lights began to flicker, the pile of cabbage leaves began to shimmy and shake and up rose a life-size Cabbage Patch Kid! IT WAS MY AUNT CACK!!! I can’t recall the rest of the skit, though I remember everyone loving it, but I distinctly remember bursting with pride that my aunt was the actress!

Another time, at another Corpus Christi pageant, Aunt Cack and her friend Phyllis Morrissey played a huge joke on everyone. Her friend was a famous Newfoundland singer with a powerful and beautiful voice. Suffice to say, Aunt Cack wasn’t known for her singing abilities. But that night Aunt Cack stood out front of the red curtain with a microphone and began to “sing” “Danny Boy”… only it was actually her friend singing from behind the curtain. Phyllis told me she’s never sung so hard in her life, she belted it out to the rafters, like her life depended on it. She hit notes she could hardly believe herself! The two of them hammed it up so hard that everyone was crying with laughter!

Mary and Cack were such fun people and such kind friends. You just knew you could be completely yourself with them; they were very accepting but they also never held back on telling you exactly what they thought. Honest and open friendship was very important to all the Dalys. If you were kind, smart, and loved to laugh, then you were welcome in their home. You could come in and share your troubles in confidence, and you were accepted for who you were.

May the Road Rise Up to Meet You

It's getting on time to say goodbye. I hope you enjoyed meeting my great-aunties and -uncles, Kitty and Daniel, and all the rest. There are so many stories, it's hard to pick which ones to tell.

The most important part of this story, though, isn't hard to pick: despite its many struggles and hardships, this family stayed together. They figured out ways to make their homes and lives suit them, and they built a wonderful community of friends and family whom they loved dearly and who loved them in return. Those six great-aunties and great-uncles were small in stature but not in spirit, smarts, or personality. Like my great-grandmother Kitty, they had a wonderful bigness to them. And they taught me that whatever challenge might come my way, I could keep looking for the joy and beauty and fun in life. I'm grateful to have been born into such a family. To be their Mo'Cuishle (that's Irish for pulse of my heart, or darling). They will always, ever be, the pulse of my heart as well.

All those years ago, when the archbishop asked her what she thought God wanted her to do about her small children, Kitty Daly said that "if a place could be made for her children, it would be," and then she and Daniel and all their family made sure that a place *was* made—a place that welcomed and nurtured children of all shapes, sizes, and abilities, that welcomed friends and visitors of every ilk, that welcomed priests and poets, that welcomed grandchildren and great grandchildren. They knew that there is room for everyone if we all make a little room for each other.

Back: Kitty
Bottom: Cack, Rose, unknown, Mary, Mike, Ann, unknown

Gordon Daly, Uncle Mike Bishop, Bill Daly

Joe Daly

Back: Kitty
Bottom: Mike Bishop, Mike, Theresa, Bill, Cack, Daniel, Rose-Marie, Rose
Floor: Mary

Activities

How to:

SPIN NICKLES (like my great-uncle Mike)

You may need an expert to help you as you learn. There is a bit of a trick to this...

* Put the nickel on its edge on the table. It has to be a hard surface, no tablecloths.

* Hold the nickel between your left thumb and right index finger and pull the two towards each other quickly to flick the nickel into a spin! Keep it on the table, don't let it pop up or fly away.

* Once you get the hang of it, it's great fun and helps pass the time. Why not have a nickel spinning competition with your cousin or a friend?

GROW AFRICAN VIOLETS ON YOUR WINDOWSILL (like my great-grandmother Kitty)

These beautiful plants are not native to Newfoundland and Labrador or elsewhere in North America, but lots of people have one. The trick to keeping these velvety beauties happy is that they must be watered from the bottom. I bet you didn't know that!

* Keep them in gentle sunlight and give them a drink once a week, and they will bloom for you.

* Pour the water in a saucer and lay the flower pot in it for twenty minutes—that's how you do it.

* If you are so inclined, you could sprinkle Holy Water on them every evening before you go to bed like Kitty did. Good night and God bless ye!

MAKE A JARDINEER OR JARDINIÈRE (like my great-aunt Rose)

You will need:
—a stack of old greeting cards or magazines
—a pair of scissors
—glue
—old x-ray film, a flexible transparency sheet, or something similar to make the base and sides of the jardinière
—a needle and yarn or embroidery thread

* Carefully cut out any flowers (or rainbows or ducks or balloons, whatever strikes your fancy) from the cards and lay them to the side.

* Cut the x-ray film into five pieces, one for the base and four for the sides.

* Sew the edges of the x-ray film together to make the container.

* Glue your flowers (or whatever you chose to cut out) in an artful way on each side of the container and let dry.

Voilà! Une jardinière!

WRITE A SONG (like all those musical Dalys)

I wrote the song "Kitty Darling" for our stage version of this story…I love writing songs and you will too!

* First, think of the situation you would like to describe. List out all the things you know are true about the situation. Be specific. For example, "Mo'Cuishle" is what my poppy called us, so I made sure to put that in there.

* Then, think of symbols or images that would fit your song. I knew Daniel was big and strong and could build anything, even a house, and that Kitty was a great gardener. Also, at that time people like Kitty and Daniel needed to be able to grow their own food because where they lived there was no such thing as a grocery store.

* Think of lots of different ways of describing the person or situation, like Kitty Darlin, Kitty Dear, Kitty Dove…

* Now, line up all your words in such a way that you are speaking honestly from one person's perspective. In this case, Daniel wants to convince Kitty that he's the best man for her to marry (it worked!) because he is capable of creating a solid life but also because he's poetic and romantic.

* This part might sound like a challenge, but you can do it—pick a tune from your head. Keep it simple at first; you can add more later. Hum some notes and try to fit them to the words. Give it a chance. You might think it's not very good at first but let it settle.

* Sing it a lot to yourself, and then, when you are ready, sing it to your friends to see what they think. Just one or two, no need for a concert. And there you have it! You are on your way!

MAKE A FAMILY TREE (OR BRAMBLE)

* Start with a big piece of paper; at the very top, write the names of your great-grandparents (if you know who they are). For example: Kitty Ryan + Daniel Daly

* Draw a line down from the great-grandparents to list their children's names underneath. Example: Bill, Mike, Ann, Peter, Rose, Theresa, Tom, Gordon, Joe, Mary, Cack, Daniel

* You might need a lot of room on the paper, and you may need to tidy it up again later, but pick one of the children and add the person they had children with. So my example is Pop: Bill Daly + Mary Quilty

* Then draw a line down from THAT couple, and list any children they had. Example: Catherine Ann, Rose Marie

* Draw another line down from one of those people and add their children. Example: Catherine Ann grew up to be Kay Haynes (she's my mom!) so a line under my mom goes to my brothers and sister and me: Arthur, Maria, Diana, Bill.

* We can even go one further and a line from Arthur goes to his children, Annabelle and Benjamin. No more lines for them yet because they are just little kiddos now, the youngest in our family.

Please note: Lots of families have lots of different structures. Some folks have two moms or two dads or two dads and a mom and step-parents and half-brothers and half-sisters and kids who are adopted in and adopted out and some folks separate and get new partners and oh! The possibilities are endless! That's why sometimes I call it a bramble: it can get really tricky, a little tangly, but that's what keeps it interesting!

Glossary

Archbishop: powerful head of a diocese, or geographic region designated by the church. Archbishops hold great sway in the Roman Catholic Church, and at the time had much to say about how their parishioners lived their lives.

Autodidact: someone who learns things without the help of a teacher, and so is self-taught

The Bay Taxi: a service offering transportation for people in remote outport communities to and from St. John's

Cabbage Patch Kids: stuffed dolls with plastic heads and faces, and yarn hair. These were among the most popular toys in North America in 1980s.

"Danny Boy": one of the most popular Irish ballads ever. Some people think it's about a mother singing to her son who is going off to war; others think it is about Irish emigration, or leaving Ireland to live somewhere else.

Dispensation: permission given by someone in authority, like an archbishop, to go against the usual rules of the Catholic Church

Divilskin: a little spritely troublemaker

Drills: grooves made into the soil into which seeds are sown

Faeries: little magical folk who live in the in-between world. Faeries could lead you astray and take you off into their enchanted world. In Newfoundland, faeries tend to be tricksy or even malevolent. If you were "taken by the faeries" then you were never fully focussed or present in the human world. One means of protection from the faeries is to put bread in your pockets, especially if you are walking anywhere at night.

Fish Flakes: a platform built on poles and spread with boughs for drying and salting cod

Filleting: removing the bones from a fish and cutting it into strips

Gordon Lightfoot: one of Canada's most successful singer-songwriters of the 20th century. His music influenced generations and was a favourite in the Daly household.

The Lady of Shalott: a woman, in a poem by Alfred Lord Tennyson, who lived in a tower and could only observe the outside world through a mirror. When she turned to engage with the world without it, the mirror cracked and she died.

The Lancers: a set dance, also known as a square dance or quadrille, usually for four couples. The dance has five movements or figures. The figures of set dances often have local names like "through the woods" where everyone passes each other in the circle, briefly linking hands as they cross each other, or "men step out" where the man from each couple steps to the centre and step dances on the spot with each man from the other couples in a friendly, gentlemanly way. Set dances were extremely popular in Newfoundland at the turn of the 20th century. More recently, folklorists and dance enthusiasts have collected and recorded the dances, and taught them to their contemporaries, to help preserve them.

Little People: a term for a person of short stature, who has a medical or genetic condition that results in them not growing any taller than 4'10". In the past, people of short stature were called dwarves; now we seek to use terms that are more inclusive.

Sometimes the limbs and torsos of people of short stature are disproportionate to the rest of their bodies; sometimes they are not. Sometimes they will also have another genetic condition, like my great-aunt Rose who likely had osteogenesis imperfecta.

MENSA: an international group whose only criterion is exceptional intelligence. Members must score within the upper 2% of a special intelligence test.

Mo'Cuishle: Irish Gaelic for "my darling," "my blood," "pulse of my heart," "blood of my veins"

Newfoundland: a large island off the east coast of the North American mainland. The island has long been the home of several Indigenous peoples. Its wealth of codfish attracted fishermen from many European countries, and as a result for much of the last 500 years, fishing has been central to its economy. It was colonized by both the British and the French, and now is part of Newfoundland and Labrador, a province of Canada.

Osteogenesis Imperfecta: translates as "imperfect bone formation," also known as brittle bone syndrome. This is a group of genetic disorders that results in various complications including short stature and bones that are fragile and break easily.

Purity Syrup: a delicious syrup used to flavour water or ginger ale. It is produced in St. John's, NL at the Purity Factory and is a favourite part of Christmas. It comes in a rainbow of flavours, including strawberry, raspberry, cherry, orange, lemon, and lime.

Rocky Marciano: an American professional boxer who competed from 1947 to 1955, and held the world heavy weight title from 1952 to 1956

Rosary (Hail Mary/ Glorious Mystery): a special sequence of prayers that devout Catholics say daily. There are so many repetitions in each section that a special set of beads, rosary beads, are used to help keep track of where the person praying is in the prayer. Essentially it is a meditation for each "Glorious Mystery" of the Roman Catholic Faith. Often one person leads it in a call-and-response fashion. The leader will say the first part of the prayer and the others will join in with the second part.

Sheila's Brush: a snow storm that occurs around the spring equinox, shortly after St. Patrick's Day. In Newfoundland, it is usually the last big storm of winter. Stories vary, but Sheila is said to be St. Patrick's housekeeper, or sister, or mother, and is sweeping away the old season—sometimes with gusto, sometimes in anger.

Skeletal Dysplasia: a category of rare genetic disorders that cause abnormal development of a baby's bones, joints, and cartilage. While skeletal dysplasia affects different parts of the body in different children, most often the legs and arms, ribcage, skull, and/or spine will be affected.

St. Mary's Bay: the most southern and eastern of Newfoundland's major bays

Tommy Makem, the Clancey Brothers, the Sons of Erin, the Carlton Show Band: bands and musicians who were hugely popular in the 1970s and played a large role in the "Irish Revival" re-popularizing Irish music that had almost passed into obscurity. They were fun and romantic, and often incorporated live actors and dancers in their shows. They would do live stage shows and TV specials. The Dalys were all big fans, but none bigger than Mary and Cack.

Town: anywhere that is not the Bay…but for us, it means St. John's

Waterloo Stove: a brand of cast-iron cook stove that was fueled by woodfire

How this book came to be

This book is based on the live stage show "If A Place Could Be Made" by the Daly Family Collective (which is made up of Louise Moyes, Anne Troake, and me). Initially a Docudance project and created with Docudance methods, "If A Place Could Be Made" is the source of almost all of the research and the first draft for this book. I used the script from the show as a starting point for the narrative, and indeed, some passages are directly from the show, which was written collectively.

The stories are true and they belong to my family, but they would not have been presented in this way if Louise Moyes hadn't applied her tremendous insight, dedication, and talent into collecting these stories, collaborating with Anne Troake and me, and turning them into her signature style of performance art, a live Docudance production. In the show, Louise and I tell some of these stories onstage, and others as well, while Anne guides the flow and content, through text, songs, audio recordings, photographs, linocut prints, and contemporary dance. Ours was truly a collective creation with contributions from our friends and colleagues, sound and light designers Lori Clarke and Phil Winters too.

It still amazes me that I have friends as wildly creative, sensitive, fierce, and caring as Anne and Louise, and I am forever grateful to them for including me on this journey with them. I believe in my heart that all of my late family would be touched and chuffed that so many people respected and cared about them enough to make this show. I know that they would have LOVED Louise and Anne, and that Louise and Anne would have loved them.

Both the show and this book are a testament about living life with generous and open hearts. Indeed, there was almost always someone in the audience of these performances who wanted to stay and chat afterwards, and let us know how the Dalys touched their lives.

Mary-Ellen Wright shared her knowledge of outport Newfoundland in the early development phase of the project, and when asked about what most folks did with children with disabilities, she offered that the general thought was, rather than sending them away, "If a place could be made for them, it would be". Hence the title of our show. The show was originally produced by the Resource Centre for the Arts Theatre; the Daly Family Collective remains grateful for development contributions from the St. John's Arts and Culture Centre, ArtsNL, and the Canada Council for the Arts. "The Little Show That Could" has travelled in cars, boats, and planes, and has played in St. John's, Gander, a TON of schools in Newfoundland and Labrador (after which we held workshops with the students about equity and inclusion and making their own stories come to life), Ottawa, and New York City. What would my great-aunties and -uncles have thought of their story travelling so far and welcoming so many?

Acknowledgements

Wonderfully big thanks, of course, to Louise Moyes, Anne Troake, Lori Clarke, Phil Winters, and everyone who helped with the theatrical version of this story. Further acknowledgements go to my mother, Kay Haynes, and her sister, Rose Marie Coady (and Uncle Ed Coady too!), for sharing their personal memories with us on video and audio. Mom helped me greatly with missing details for this book version of the story. Our cousins, the Bishops are also part of this grand adventure. Susan Pike, Sharon Bishop, Janet Bishop, Judy Bishop, Terry Bishop Stirling, David Bishop, and Michele Butler are my great-aunt Theresa's children and were raised by the family the same way Mom and Aunt Rose were. They are there in every story I tell, as are all of their children. The Bishops contributed hugely to the project with interviews, audio recordings, photographs, and feedback, and for that I am eternally grateful. Chris Brookes quite skillfully managed to record our very large, very loud family storytelling night and for that he deserves a prize.

Speaking of prizes, we won the jackpot with Marnie Parsons. Her contribution to the cultural landscape of Newfoundland and Labrador is as immense as her patience. She saw our show and then approached me to turn it into a book, and I am so grateful for her guidance and editing skills.

The generation of cousins that I grew up with are: Krista Pike, Julia Pike, David Pike, Erinne Kearsey, Cindi Kearsey, Adam Kearsey, Terri Lynn Kearsey, Andrea Moores, Matthew Moores, Andrew Mefford, Lyndsay Bishop, Heather-Leah Bishop, Lydia Bishop, Garry Bishop, Katie Bishop, Sarah Stirling, Lori Coady, Stephen Coady, Jill Coady. My own dear brothers and sister are Arthur Haynes, Maria Haynes, and Bill Haynes. How lucky I am to have the likes of you as my siblings? I love you to pieces. Though I had to choose my lens to tell the stories through, they are just as much yer legacies as mine.

This book was designed by Veselina Tomova of Vis-à-Vis Graphics, St. John's, NL, and printed in Canada.

9781927917848

Running the Goat, Books & Broadsides gratefully acknowledges support for its publishing activities from Newfoundland and Labrador's Department of Tourism, Culture, Arts and Recreation through its Publishers Assistance Program; the Department of Canadian Heritage through the Canada Book Fund; and the Canada Council for the Arts, through its Literary Publishing Projects Fund.

Canada Council for the Arts | Conseil des arts du Canada

Funded by the Government of Canada
Financé par le gouvernement du Canada

Running the Goat Books & Broadsides Inc.
General Delivery/54 Cove Road
Tors Cove, Newfoundland and Labrador A0A 4A0
www.runningthegoat.com